AC 7793

MW01223095

Date Due

FEB 2 5			
NOV 2 2 2004			
NOV 2 9 2004			

Albert McDonald

FOCUS ON
WEST GERMANY

Hamish Hamilton · London

The author and publishers would like to thank the following
for permission to reproduce photographs: Allan Cash Ltd 6
(left), 31 (right); Susan Griggs Photographic Library 21 (right);
The John Hillelson Agency 1, 3, 17 (top), 25 (right); Spectrum
Colour Library 6 (right), 7, 8 (left), 10, 11 (left) 18 (top and
bottom), 19, 22, 24, 25 (left); Tony Stone Photolibrary–London
cover, 15, 29; Christa Stadtler 17 (bottom), 27 (right); ZEFA 8
(right), 9, 11 (right), 12, 13, 20, 21 (left), 23, 26, 28. The
photographs on pages 27 (left), 31 (left), are reproduced by
kind permission of the author.

Design by Andrew Shoolbred

Map by Tony Garrett

Illustrations by Louis Mackay, Linda Rogers Associates

First published in Great Britain 1985 by
Hamish Hamilton Children's Books
Garden House, 57–59 Long Acre, London, WC2E 9JZ
Copyright © 1985 by Albert McDonald
All rights reserved

British Library Cataloguing in Publication Data
McDonald, Albert
Focus on West Germany.—(Focus on)
1. Germany (West)—Social life and customs
— Juvenile literature
I. Title
93.087'8   DD260.3
ISBN 0-241-11480-2

Printed in Italy by
New Interlitho S.p.A.

Cover: A brightly painted church below the
Bavarian Alps at Ramsau. Village churches
are well cared for and are often beautifully
decorated inside. In country areas tiny white
painted churches are important meeting
places for families from the surrounding
farms.

Previous page: Flats and apartments jostle for
space in West Berlin. More than two million
people live and work in the city, but
building space is scarce within its tightly
drawn boundary. Houses are expensive and
flats are often designed to be as small as
possible in order to save space.

Fresh, locally grown vegetables on sale in ▶
Regensburg market are likely to have been
harvested only a few hours before, on a
family farm close to the city. It is often the
farmer's wife who looks after the planting
and harvesting of root crops for market. No
wonder many wives are proud of what
eventually appears on their stalls.

Contents

Introducing West Germany

Modern West Germany is one of the youngest countries in Europe. It was formed at the end of the Second World War, in 1945, when the old German Empire, which had covered most of central Europe, was divided among the USSR, Poland and two new German states. The smallest of these became East Germany (the DDR); the largest became the Bundesrepublik Deutschland. In English this means the Federal Republic of Germany, but usually the country is simply known as West Germany. Today, more than sixty million people live in West Germany, fifteen million more than in 1945.

The country

Modern West Germany covers almost a quarter of a million square kilometres and, despite having lost land after the war, is still the third largest country in Europe. It stretches more than 700 kilometres from the coastlines of the North Sea and the Baltic to the borders of Switzerland and Austria in the south; and almost 400 kilometres from the frontiers of the Netherlands, Belgium, Luxembourg and France to the DDR and Czechoslovakia in the east. Its varied landscapes include sweeping sandy beaches, rolling farmland, gentle wooded hills cut by swiftly flowing rivers, and towering snow-covered alpine peaks.

Government

Every four years West Germans elect their Bundestag, or Federal Parliament, which meets in Bonn to discuss and decide upon important national affairs. But they are also fiercely proud of ten powerful Länder, or regional governments. Each Land, or state, has its own special character: Bremen and Hamburg are international ports; Schleswig-Holstein and Lower Saxony are agricultural areas; and North-Rhine Westphalia is an industrial region.

Further south, the Rhineland Palatinate has a fairy-tale landscape of ruined castles and sweeping vineyards; Hessen has wooded mountains and stately farmhouses; and Baden-Württemberg has pretty, welcoming towns. The Saarland is an industrial region of coal-mines and steel works. Bavaria, the largest Land of all, is one of West Germany's most popular holiday regions.

Cities and towns

Bonn, the capital city

Bonn is a small town on the banks of the River Rhine, and the home of West Germany's government, the Bundestag. It only became the seat of government at the end of the Second World War, when Germany and the old imperial capital of Berlin were divided between West Germany and DDR.

Nowadays, Bonn has an impressive parliament building, new court houses, modern office blocks and many new hotels, restaurants and shops. Yet it still keeps its small-town atmosphere. The side-streets are lined with shops selling clothes, shoes and fruit. Florists, greengrocers and cafés spill out on to the city's pavements and fringe its small neat squares.

The quiet, secluded garden of Beethoven's house, now a museum, in Bonn.

Beethoven, one of West Germany's most famous composers, was born in Bonn in 1770 and tourists still visit his house, which has been converted into an attractive little museum. But most visitors quickly pass through the city to the more popular attractions of nearby Koblenz and Cologne. Bonn remains a quiet efficient town where government administrators and local townspeople live and work.

Bonn's streets still have the atmosphere of a friendly market town.

Münster

More than 160 kilometres further north the pleasant market town of Münster is more typical of West Germany's smaller cities. Two hundred years ago, the centre of Münster was still a tight cluster of half-timbered houses and narrow streets, surrounded by a massive medieval wall, neat strips of garden and sweeping grain fields. Then in the nineteenth and early twentieth centuries, small industries began to replace the merchant houses and the town's character began to change.

There were even greater changes during the Second World War when Münster, like many other West German towns, was badly damaged by heavy fighting and bombing. However, large areas have now been reconstructed: the ruined cathedral and many of the best medieval merchant houses have been rebuilt, and less attractive parts of the town have been replaced by bright modern buildings. Stretches of the town walls have been knocked down and replaced by wide wooded walks.

Modern Münster is still a friendly market town. The cathedral square has a thriving market with dozens of stalls selling locally grown fruit and vegetables. Farmers bring in their produce to sell, have lunch in the town's cafés, shop in the narrow streets or visit their children in Münster's famous university. Everywhere, there is the sound of bells: thousands of jingling bicycle bells, church bells and loud cathedral bells which ring out across the old town on Sundays and church festivals.

Winding market streets and medieval houses were rebuilt after much of Münster was destroyed during the Second World War.

Nuremberg at Christmas
One of the most exciting times to visit the city of Nuremberg in Bavaria is three weeks before Christmas. This is when the city holds its annual Christkindlesmarkt (Christmas market).

Christmas is a very special time in West Germany, and many families visit the Christkindlesmarkt in preparation for the holiday. The city streets are crowded with stalls and booths selling food, drinks and gifts. There is always lots of beer, hot spiced wine, sausages and spicy, sugar-glazed gingerbread biscuits.

Village life

West Germany's villages vary greatly from the north to the south. Along the River Mosel the wine villages of Piesport, Bernkastel-Kues and Zeil are mazes of narrow cobbled streets, lined with half-timbered houses which open on to attractive squares. The villages of southern Bavaria are neat clusters of sparkling alpine chalets, while those on the northern lowlands, close to the North Sea, are of a sturdy, more practical appearance.

Impressive half-timbered buildings overlook the village square of Mittenberg am Main.

No matter where the villages are, they tend to be clean, fresh and well-ordered. For most West Germans, neatness and tidiness is a way of life. They wear better clothes, enjoy better food, take more exotic holidays and have a higher standard of living than many of their European neighbours – and this wealth is reflected in their villages.

At home

Villages are pleasant places to live and houses are usually well-built and cared for. Outside walls are often plastered and painted in attractive pastel shades.

A neat well-ordered village on the northern island of Borkum.

In southern Germany many villagers still decorate the outsides of their homes with colourful wall paintings of religious or hunting scenes.

In most villages homes are warm and comfortable. Almost all have double, or even triple, glazing, central heating, and rolling steel shutters, which keep rooms cool in summer and warm in winter. Village shops are bright and cheerful, and most larger villages still have their own outdoor markets selling locally grown fruit and vegetables.

Church and school

For many West German families, life still centres around the local village church – which is often the oldest building in the community. Apart from providing a place for worship and village activities, churches often run kindergartens for local pre-school children between the ages of three and six years.

The pretty village church of Speiden im Allageu on the fringe of the Alps.

From the age of six, all village children attend the local primary school, or 'Grundschule'. They stay here for between four and six years (depending on where they live) and are taught a wide variety of subjects. These include reading, writing and arithmetic, and often science, German history and local geography as well. Some schools also teach a foreign language.

Young West Germans take their lessons seriously but school is far from being all work and no play. Art, handicrafts and sports are part of every village school's curriculum. Some schools in alpine areas arrange ski-ing lessons and many have swimming, football and archery lessons.

The future?

Villages are often very pleasant places to live, but after school, college or university, people often find it difficult to find suitable jobs nearby. Many leave their village to look for work in a town or city. Villages in poorer areas are getting smaller. Many young families have moved away, schools have fewer pupils and shops have closed. Some little villages along the Rhine, and in the mountain areas, are now almost deserted for most of the year. They only become busy when visitors come to stay during the summer tourist season.

On the farm

There are many different types of farm in West Germany. In the foothills of the Alps, and along the fringes of the North Sea, there are lots of 'pastoral' farms. These are mainly used for grazing cattle and sheep. Arable farms, which are almost entirely devoted to crops, are limited to a few areas which have a mild climate, fertile soil, and land level enough for modern farm machinery. Most farms in West Germany are mixed, combining both arable and pastoral farming. In mountain areas, mixed farms may also include areas of woodland.

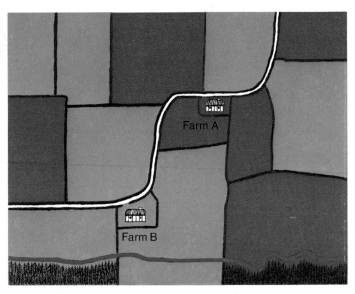

Farm A's fields are separated from each other by Farm B's fields.

Mixed farms

A typical mixed farm in West Germany covers between 20 and 50 hectares. This is small by West European standards, and tiny in comparison with farms in North America, South Africa, Australia and New Zealand. Such a small farm is difficult to run profitably, particularly as its small irregular fields are divided from one another by land belonging to neighbouring farms. This strange pattern has developed over the last six hundred years as farmers have died and their land has been divided amongst a number of sons.

Using the land

In order to overcome these problems, farmers make the most of their scattered plots. Fields in valley bottoms are often flooded in winter and too wet

Harvesting grain above the Rhine.

Cattle grazing the lush green grass of a Bavarian valley.

for cereal crops like wheat and barley, but they can be planted with grass to provide pasture for beef and dairy cattle. Hilly land with sandy soil is often too infertile for crops and too dry for good pasture, and so this is often used as rough grazing for sheep or planted as woodland. Only the best, most fertile land is used for crops. Many farms grow oats, rye, sugar-beet and potatoes, although the most common crops are wheat and barley.

Smaller farms

Every year, farm machinery, chemicals and fertilizers become more expensive, and many small farms find it difficult to make any profit at all. Some farmers add to their income by working in nearby towns and only tend their land in evenings and at weekends. Many more have sold their scattered fields to larger neighbouring farms.

Changing crops

Larger farms can afford to grow a much wider range of crops. If the soil is fertile, many farmers produce apples, cherries, pears and soft fruits, such as strawberries, which can be sold for a good price. They may also breed pigs, chickens, turkeys, geese and ducks in large specially built sheds. This is a very efficient type of farming because it needs very little land. Factory farming units can be built on the most infertile areas, pigs and poultry can be fed on wheat and barley grown on the farm, and animals or birds can be sold when prices are at their highest.

Pigs are kept on many German farms.

Beer and wine

Beer has been brewed in Germany since well before Roman times, and is still one of the country's most popular drinks. All beers are made from wheat or barley with hops, but each beer has its own special flavour. Almost every major town and city in West Germany has at least one brewery, and the largest towns, such as Berlin or Munich, have several.

Different beers

German beers are often named after the town where they were made. Berliner beer comes from Berlin, Bremer from Bremen, Düssel from Düsseldorf, and so on. Many beers are still produced by small local breweries which only brew enough to satisfy local demand. But the most popular beers are made in large industrial breweries on a much bigger scale. Some, such as Dortmunder Union, are sold in towns all over West Germany, as well as in France, Switzerland and Italy. In these countries, German beers are often more popular than locally produced ones. Some West German beers are so popular that they are exported in bottles, cans, and even road tankers.

These include:

 Berliner Kindl, which is brewed in West Berlin using only the finest malt and hops;

 Holstein Diat Pils Lager, which is strong in alcohol;

 Löwenbräu, which has been made in Munich since 1338;

 Meister Pils, which is brewed in Kassel to an old Bavarian recipe.

Enjoying a glass of refreshing beer.

Harvesting wine grapes in Rheinhessen.

Wine

West Germans also value their wines. Neatly planted vineyards stretch along the banks of the Rivers Rhine, Ahr, Mosel, Nahe, Neckar and Main, and on the higher land either side of these rivers. White Riesling grapes ripen during the long warm summers, and are ready for picking in late autumn before the first frosts arrive to spoil the fruit.

Once, an army of workers trod the grapes to extract juice ready for making into wine. But they have long since been replaced by modern industrial machinery. Now the grapes are crushed by heavy steel rollers, then automatically loaded into stainless steel tanks and squeezed dry. The grape juice is pumped into vats and yeast is added. This changes some of the natural sugar in the grape juice into alcohol – and so the juice is turned into wine. In the modern wineries of the Main, Mosel and middle Rhine all this can be done by two or three people pressing buttons in a central control room.

West Germans are proud of their beer and wine. The first brew from a new season's hops or a new vintage of wine has always been a time for celebrations and festivals, and hundreds of beer and wine festivals are held in West Germany each year. By far the largest is the annual Octoberfest in Munich. The city's seven largest breweries set up gigantic beer tents which can hold up to 5000 people each. Chicken and oxen are spit-roasted in the open air, there are colourful processions, brass bands and numerous side-shows. The entire city centre takes on an exciting fairground atmosphere.

Wine labels
West Germany has very strict wine laws. They ensure that every wine bottle label includes detailed information about the quality of the wine inside.

Deutscher Tafelwein is ordinary table wine. It may be made from grapes grown in several different part of West Germany.

Q.b.A. means the wine is of good quality. It must have been made from certain types of grapes grown in the region named on the label.

Q.m.P. means the wine is one of the best produced in West Germany.

13

Food

First-time visitors to West Germany are often pleasantly surprised by the hearty and satisfying food to be found there. Even in small hotels, tourist restaurants, and motorway service areas, meals are simply cooked, tasty and very filling. But visitors who only eat in these places might think that West German food is limited to a small number of dishes. In fact, there are many more than the tourist favourites of brown bread, pickled herrings, fried chicken, spicy sausages, one or two savoury meat dishes, and magnificent cream cakes.

Outside the main tourist areas, cooking is much more interesting and varied. Although there are striking variations in food from one region to another, as a general rule people in the north eat large amounts of fish, vegetables and potatoes, while those in the south prefer thick soups, veal steaks and pasta dishes.

Northern fish dishes

In the far north, close to the sea and around the ports of Bremen, Hamburg and Lübeck, there are many different fish dishes. Eels, lobsters, sprats and trout are all common, although herring is the most popular. It can be baked, fried or pickled with onions and herbs. A traditional way of preparing herring is to preserve it in salty water for about eight weeks until the flavour begins to develop and mature. Then the still raw herring is served with a thick sauce of cream, apple and raw onions, and side dishes of raw onion and pickled beetroot.

beetroot / raw herring / onion

Ham and cheese

Further south, in Lower Saxony, roast lamb, pickled pork and savoury sausage are served with huge basins of mashed potato and sweet and sour cabbage. A little further west, in North-Rhine Westphalia, delicious cottage-smoked hams, cheeses and sausages are popular. These are best eaten with hunks of fresh farmhouse bread and butter.

Along the Rhine, there is pickled beef, jugged pork and fresh river fish, as well as many regional specialities. One of the most popular is a dish called Heaven and Earth. This is made from a smooth mixture of potatoes, apples, black sausage and onion, which are fried together over a hot flame to make a warm winter meal. The recipe below tells you how to make another German dish.

A West German salad to make at home
(For 2–3 people)
Many West German dishes combine sweet and sharp tastes. This salad uses Bierwurst, a rough-textured pork sausage flavoured with spices.

You will need:

Salad
220 grams of German Bierwurst, sliced and cut into 1cm strips.
1 ripe juicy apple, pared, cored and cut into cubes.
6 small slices of pickled beetroot cut into 1cm strips.

Salad dressing
½ teaspoon of brown sugar.
1 tablespoon of olive oil.
½ teaspoon of mild German mustard.

Put the salad ingredients in a bowl and mix together. In a separate bowl, mix the sugar, oil and mustard. Pour the dressing over the salad to make a tasty snack.

Pork and sausages

In Hessen, the speciality is pork. It is cooked in every possible way – pickled, fried, roasted, boiled, baked – and, most famous of all, made into Frankfurter sausages. These are cooked slowly over wood fires to give them a fine smoky flavour. They are eaten with pickled cabbage and potato salad, or in vegetable soup.

In Baden-Württemberg and Bavaria, in the far south, the style of cooking is more elaborate. Meat dishes of pork, beef and veal are often served with dumplings, pasta and many different types of bread. Hundreds of different kinds of sausage are made, the most famous of which are Nürnberger Rostbratwürste. These are made of pork, and roasted over charcoal fires during Nuremberg's annual open-air Christmas fair.

A wide range of sausages cooking on a Nuremberg hot dog stand.

Industry and power

West Germany's industries are among the most successful in Europe. Large iron and steel plants, chemical refineries, engineering factories and many others make it a rich powerful nation.

Traditional industries

Many of West Germany's heavy industries are still based on rich reserves of coal, metal ores, and minerals. A lot of these industries developed in the middle of the last century. As they grew, Germany changed from a collection of small states, which measured their wealth in harvests of wheat and rye, to a mighty industrial empire based on coal and iron. Germany's production of iron, steel, ships, railway locomotives, steam engines and industrial machinery was only matched by that of Great Britain and the USA.

These heavy industries were close to the mines which provided the raw materials, and above the coalfields which supplied the fuel. Since the end of the Second World War, they have been almost totally rebuilt, although they are still grouped together on the iron and coalfields of the Ruhr and the Saar, and close to the mineral deposits scattered across the southern edge of the North German Plain.

More than two million people still work in West Germany's heavy industries. They produce special steels, chemicals, cars, trucks, ships and a wide range of industrial machinery which is exported to all parts of the world.

West German cars
Modern West German factories produce more than 4 million cars every year. Most of these are bought by Germans, while the rest are exported to countries all over the world. Find out how popular West German cars are where you live. Look out for:

 Volkswagen, made at Wolfsburg in Lower Saxony.

 Opel, made at Russelsheim and Bochum.

 Mercedes-Benz, made at Sindelfingen and Untertürkheim in Bavaria.

The Krupps steel works at Rheinhäuser.

New industries

A large number of modern new industries have also developed since the end of the Second World War. Clocks, cameras, musical instruments, televisions, hi-fi sets, computers and videos are just some of the goods they export. West Berlin, in particular, also produces large amounts of modern fashionable clothes. Expensive glass and high quality ceramics are made in

BMW cars near the end of the assembly line in Munich.

the south, and almost every West German town has dozens of small workshops making local handicrafts – everything from furniture to toys.

Power

Originally, West Germany's rapid industrial growth was powered by its vast coal reserves. The coalfields all played their part in fuelling ships, driving steam engines and supplying power stations with the energy to produce electricity. Nowadays, most of West Germany's best coal has been mined, and what remains is expensive to dig out. As a result, new, less costly fuels are being used more and more. Natural gas, imported oil, hydro-electric power and nuclear energy are all rapidly growing in importance.

New problems

However, post-war rebuilding and rapid industrial growth have also brought problems. People have tended to move into successful industrial areas, so causing shortages in housing and school places, and overcrowding of vital services such as hospitals. Some areas, such as those along the borders with Denmark, Czechoslovakia and the Netherlands, have become almost empty as people have moved away to richer parts of the country. Unemployment is a problem for many people who live in northern Bavaria and parts of the Rhineland Palatinate.

Water transport

Inland waterways carry almost one quarter of all goods transported in West Germany. Barges, push-tugs and even small freighters can penetrate deep into the industrial heart of the country on a well-maintained system of rivers and man-made canals.

Rivers

Rivers have been used as important routes for thousands of years. Roman galleys carried building stone, grain, wine and troops from the snow-covered Alps to the wide sandy estuaries of the North Sea. Medieval trading vessels travelled along the Rhine, Weser and Elbe. They carried silks, spices, salt, pottery, and many other goods to the thriving market towns along the river banks. Rivers have always been one of the best ways to move heavy, bulky or expensive goods through the wooded, mountainous landscape of central Germany.

The River Rhine (see also pp 20–21) was made an international waterway in 1868, so allowing vessels from all countries to journey up and down the river. Since then the Rhine and its

River barges carry heavy loads through the Rhine gorge.

A large modern canal barge carefully entering a lock on the River Main.

tributary rivers, especially the Mosel, Neckar and Main, have become busier each year. Shallow sections of the rivers have been deepened, and wide straight canals have been dug to link other industrial areas to the rivers.

Canals

Powerful diesel barges from many European countries carry heavy cargoes along West Germany's wide canals. The Mittelland Canal is one of West Germany's most important man-made waterways. It cuts across the rolling plains of northern Germany for more than 200 kilometres. Barges from the Rhine can reach the Mittelland Canal by a shorter link canal, and so carry

A laden coal barge makes its way past the vine-covered banks of the River Mosel.

oil, coal and important industrial chemicals to the cities and factories of north Germany. Barges can reach the canal from across the border with the DDR. Valuable cargoes of West German exports are sent eastwards in return for ore, chemicals, and even timber from the faraway forests of eastern Poland.

The River Mosel

Other canals and rivers link West Germany with Belgium, the Netherlands, Switzerland, Austria and Hungary. Several others, including the Main–Danube Canal, are still under construction or improvement.

One of the most recent rivers to be opened to large vessels is the River Mosel, which rises in France, passes through Luxembourg and joins the Rhine at Koblenz. The river has been dredged to prevent barges running aground on the Mosel's many sandbanks. Twelve wide modern locks have been built so that shipping can avoid the dangerous rocky rapids.

Barges loaded with coal, oil, and sometimes even wine, move up and down the busy river, past towering castles, sweeping vineyards and attractive villages. Although the Mosel valley has always been a busy route between Germany and France, the opening of the river to shipping has made it a vital link between these two countries.

The River Rhine

The River Rhine carries more shipping than any other river in the world. Powerful self-propelled diesel barges jostle for space with neatly painted tourist launches. Tugs chug up and down the river, pushing as many as eight heavily-loaded barges before them. Bulk cargoes of oil, coal, building materials, chemicals and steel are shipped from port to port, linking the industries of West Germany with those of Switzerland and the Netherlands.

Smaller rivers and canals bring in more goods from France, Luxembourg, Belgium and the Danube countries (Austria, Czechoslovakia, Hungary, Yugoslavia, Rumania and Bulgaria). Other types of transport also use the Rhine valley as a link between north and south. Where the valley narrows into a steep gorge, motorways, electrified railways and oil pipelines crowd the narrow river banks.

The Ruhr

On its way to the sea, the River Rhine flows past some of the richest manufacturing regions of West Germany. One of these is the Ruhr area. It takes its name from the River Ruhr, which joins the Rhine 75 kilometres south of Cologne. Until 1960, coal-mining and steel-making were two of the main industries in the Ruhr–Rhine region. Duisburg-Ruhrort was an important river port where vast amounts of coal and steel were shipped along these two rivers. In the last few years coal has become less important, but new industries have been built around the river. Factories now make motor cars, television sets, radios and all sorts of modern electrical equipment.

Barges berthed on the busy river port of Duisburg–Ruhrort.

This ancient river toll house of Burg Pfalf at Kaub is now a popular tourist attraction.

Dramatic rapids at Schaffhausen, where the Rhine flows into Germany from Switzerland.

Tourism

This busy river is also at the centre of a popular tourist region. A little upstream from the Ruhr, the Rhine valley narrows into a spectacular gorge as the river cuts it way through the Rhenish slate mountains. Towering grey cliffs are crowned with romantic castles and villages, where tourists hear tales of ancient treasures, elegant counts and robber barons.

With vineyards clinging to its rocky sides, and tiny colourful villages dotted along its banks and cliffs, the Rhine gorge is one of the most attractive tourist areas in West Germany. Tour boats cruise along the river from its delta, close to Rotterdam, to dramatic waterfalls at Schaffhausen, on the border with Switzerland.

Overlooking the river, there are friendly family inns to welcome the numerous holidaymakers who come here throughout the summer. Many tourists visit the toll house of Burg Pfalf, built on a rocky island to collect river tolls over five hundred years ago. They can also see the nearby ancient castle of Rheinstein, from where there is a bird's eye view of the Rhine. One of the most impressive sights is the Lorelei Rock, which towers 132 metres above the swiftly flowing river.

Tourist attractions

Other tourist attractions on the Rhine include an ancient fortress at Koblenz, the cathedral city of Cologne, and some of the best vineyards in West Germany. No wonder West Germans are so proud of their mighty river, and for centuries have called it 'Old Father Rhine'.

Road and rail

West Germany's roads and railways have been almost totally rebuilt since the end of the Second World War. By 1945, heavy fighting had shattered railways, damaged roads and destroyed many of the country's most important bridges. Even worse, the division of the old German Empire into two new states had cut the pre-war transport network in two. So although major roads and railways between east and west were no longer needed, it was essential to build new north–south routes to link major industrial areas in the newly formed state of West Germany.

Rebuilding the railways

Once the war had ended, West Germany began to rebuild its railways. Today, most old steam locomotives have been replaced by powerful new diesel engines, and fast efficient electric trains run between the country's major cities. Old railway tracks, some of them more than a hundred years old, have been replaced by modern, high-speed railway lines. Traditional hand-operated signals have been replaced by the very latest computerised signals.

West Germany's railways are now the most modern and efficient in Europe. There are sleeper trains for long distance journeys, and most trains serve snacks and meals. The country's main cities are linked by the super-fast Trans European Express trains. These TEE trains are more expensive than other trains, and travellers must book their seats in advance. But they are

A modern train in Frankfurt.

more luxurious and offer a wide range of special services, including radio-telephones and multilingual secretaries.

One of West Germany's new motorways linking Bavaria with the Rhine.

West Germany's railways
Germany's first railway engine was the 'Adler', built by Robert Stevenson and Company in England. The Adler was sent to Germany complete with a driver, who was thought so important he was paid more than the railway company's General Manager. The first cargo to be pulled by the Adler was a shipment of beer.

On the roads

Many of West Germany's major roads have also been completely rebuilt over the last forty years, so that it now has the largest autobahn (motorway) network in western Europe. The autobahns link major cities and important industrial areas. So although railways still carry most of the heavy traffic over long distances, autobahns are preferred for smaller loads and shorter distances.

Germany's first autobahns were built in the early 1930s and, like its railways, were designed to link the imperial capital of Berlin with the distant cities of the Empire. Since the Second World War, most roads have been designed to make travel easier between north and south West Germany, although others carry international traffic through central Europe.

Set in the middle of industrial Europe, West Germany is surrounded by neighbours – Denmark, the Netherlands, Belgium, Luxembourg, France, Switzerland, Austria, Czechoslovakia and the DDR. This means that people and goods travelling between many of these countries must pass through West Germany. Apples and pears arrive from Italy via Austria; long-distance tourist coaches pass through on their way to Greece, Turkey and Yugoslavia; timber arrives from the forests of Poland; and ferries from West Germany's northern ports link the country's roads and railways to those of Great Britain, Norway, Sweden and Finland.

North Sea coasts

Busy ports, quiet sandy beaches, tourist resorts and small lonely islands are just some of the different types of scenery you might see on West Germany's North Sea coastline. From the wide sweeping estuary of the River Ems on the border with the Netherlands, the coast stretches first east and then north, past the mouths of the Rivers Weser and Elbe, to the border with Denmark more than 400 kilometres away.

Holiday-makers sunbathe on the Friesian island of Borkum.

The Friesian Islands

Between ten and twenty kilometres off the coast, the Friesian Islands lie like a long straggling necklace. They are the home of many sea-faring legends and traditions. For centuries the islanders have been boat-builders, net-makers and fishermen in the stormy waters of the North Sea. Boat-building and fishing are still the main island industries, but now tourism is also a valuable source of income. Every year, thousands of people visit the islands, attracted by the bracing sea air, long sandy beaches, pretty fishing villages and numerous health spas.

Health resorts have been built on several of the larger islands. Visitors to Sylt and Borkum can enjoy fresh sea air and health-giving mineral waters. The climate of the most easterly islands is said to be especially good for relieving hay fever and asthma.

Several of the larger islands are popular summer holiday resorts for West German families. Small hotels, guest houses and pretty beach villages increase in number each year. Some resorts have casinos, night-clubs and small local theatres, while almost all

Many Friesian islanders still make a living by fishing the waters around their islands

Hamburg is West Germany's largest and liveliest sea port.

offer sailing, swimming, wind-surfing and sail-boarding. People can also explore small sandstone coves, used by generations of smugglers, or visit nature reserves, where there are nesting sites for thousands of sea birds.

The sea ports

Even with their thousands of summer tourists, the Friesian Islands are quiet and peaceful compared with the busy bustling northern sea ports of Hamburg, Bremen and Wilhelmshaven. These large industrial cities are separated from the rest of West Germany by a wide expanse of infertile heathland, and are bypassed by the mighty trade route of the Rhine, which reaches the sea after passing through the Netherlands.

Hamburg

Like most West German towns, each port has its own special atmosphere and character. The richest and liveliest of them all is Hamburg. This is West Germany's greatest port and the home of many thriving industries based on shipbuilding, oil-refining, metal-working and chemicals.

The attractive city centre is built on either side of a wide lake on the River Alster. Sailing yachts and busy ferry boats glide to and fro across the lake, while on its banks villas and older brick-built merchant houses stand side by side with modern office blocks.

North Sea wildlife
The coastal mudbanks along the North Sea provide food for millions of sea birds. Every square metre teems with snails, crabs, mussels, starfish and many other sea creatures. Some birds, like the barnacle goose, stay for only part of the year. Others, such as the oyster-catcher, live there all year round.

Barnacle goose   Oyster-catcher

Forests

Thousands of years ago, almost all of what is now West Germany was clothed in thick forests of oak, beech and birch. Over the years, much of this woodland has been cleared to make way for farms, villages, towns and industries. Now, the forests are much smaller than they originally were, although they still cover more than one quarter of the country.

The forests are mostly found on the higher land in the southern half of the country. They cover the Rhine Highlands, the Odenwald, and the lower slopes of the Alps as they rise towards the border with Austria. On lower ground, there is the Black Forest and the Bohemian Forest.

Over the last hundred years, many areas of natural forest have been cut and replanted with faster-growing conifer trees, such as spruce, pine and fir. More than half of the forests are now 'man-made'. Large plantations are found in the southern states of Bavaria and Baden-Württemberg.

The high rolling plains of the Black Forest around the country market town of St Märgen are a patchwork of woodland and small farms. The forest here is an open and well managed one. Families combine being farmers and foresters with catering for the many thousands of tourists who visit the area each year.

Clumps of wild candytuft brighten high forest clearings on the edge of the Alps.

Forests for pleasure

West Germany's forests are attractive tourist areas where thousands of families spend weekends and holidays each year. In the summer, many of the natural woodlands in the Black Forest, the Bohemian Forest and on the lower slopes of the Alps are fresh and green, with a wide variety of different trees. Oak, beech, birch, spruce and pine grow together, as they did thousands of years ago. And in the clearings, brightly lit by shafts of spring sunshine, cowslips, bluebells and little white wood anemones bloom as soon as the winter snows have melted.

Hiking, camping and pony-trekking are popular throughout the year. Visitors to the Alpine forests and to the Black Forest can often see foxes, wildcats and large herds of wild deer. Further east, in the Bohemian Forest, hikers may even glimpse lynx, wolves and brown bears which migrate from across the nearby border with Czechoslovakia.

Forests for wealth

West Germany's vast stretches of forest are one of its most important sources of income. Germany is one of the greatest producers of timber in the EEC, with as many as one million trees being felled each year. Many of these are spruce and pine, which mature in as little as eighty years. Trees up to 40 metres high are cut throughout the year, and are carried on special transporters to large modern sawmills, which are often built in the forests themselves. Most of the timber is used for house-building, furniture, paper-making and wood-pulp.

Because timber is so important, the government takes great care to see that the forests are properly managed and protected. It owns more than half of all the forests, but even private woodland owners are encouraged to plant more trees than they cut down, and to ensure that no more forests are cleared and lost.

Specially designed tractors are used to cut timber from the Black Forest.

Mountains

The romantic image of West Germany's mountains is one of castles surrounded by steeply sloping vineyards. The brothers Grimm filled their fairy tales with villages of irregular half-timbered houses encircled by towering mountains and dark menacing forests. In fact, West Germany's mountain landscapes vary from north to south, as the ground rises from the sandy estuaries of the North Sea to the snow-covered peaks of the Alps.

The Central German Uplands

In the north, the rolling wheat fields of the North German Plain rise abruptly into a series of hills known as the

Alpine peaks near Füssen form a mountain barrier between West Germany and Austria.

Central German Uplands. These gently rise and fall about 400 metres above sea level, and are cut by deep, steep-sided valleys. Farms on these cool moist uplands are mostly devoted to cattle, although from the air the land seems thickly forested, with scattered lakes and rocky mounds marking the site of ancient extinct volcanoes.

Hessen

The mountainous region of Hessen in the east contains more woods and forests than any other part of West Germany. Yet the mountains themselves are gentle enough for families to climb on an afternoon hike.

Further south the mountains rise into steep, wooded ranges, known as the Odenwald, Black Forest, Harz and French Vosges. These are attractive hills full of surprising contrasts: wooded hills, forest walks and quiet clearings set between fertile valleys, prosperous fruit farms and fast-flowing rivers broken by the occasional waterfall. There are also many ancient castles, like the one at Heidelberg, numerous quaint half-timbered villages and a variety of health spas.

The Alps

West Germany's highest and most spectacular mountains are in the far south, where the land rises sharply up to the Zugspitze, West Germany's highest peak at 2965 metres. Thick forests give way to flower-filled alpine meadows, and then to barren snow-covered wastes. The Alps are broken by south-north valleys that have been used for thousands of years as routes between Germany and Switzerland.

Tourism

Mountains are also important tourist areas, which attract thousands of people each year. In winter, there are many sports resorts which offer skiing, tobogganing, skating and a wide range of 'après-ski' activities. At other times of the year, the mountains are popular places for hiking, pony-trekking, camping and climbing.

The Bavarian Alps

Of all the tourist attractions in the Bavarian Alps, none is more famous than the fairy-tale castle of Neuschwanstein. The castle was built by 'mad King Ludwig II of Bavaria' who ruled between 1864 and 1886.

During his reign, Ludwig II did many strange things. One night he galloped round and round his riding ring on a make-believe journey from Munich to Innsbruck. In winter, he often went on wild rides in a golden

Neuschwanstein, the 'dream castle', was built by King Ludwig II of Bavaria.

sleigh, with his coachmen dressed in the fashion of two hundred years before.

Then he decided to build himself three castles – Herrenchiemsee, Linderhof and Neuschwanstein. Of these, Neuschwanstein is the most beautiful. Set on a hill, and surrounded by woods of pine, its sparkling grey granite walls soar upwards into a forest of delicate turrets and towers. It is said that when Ludwig's government declared him mad and imprisoned him in the Schloss Berg, he drowned himself in the castle lake in sorrow at the loss of his beloved 'dream castle'.

West Berlin

West Berlin is the largest city in modern West Germany. Until the end of the Second World War in 1945, Berlin was the imperial capital of the old German Empire. This Empire stretched from the Saar coalfields in the west, only 300 kilometres from Paris, to East Prussia, only 800 kilometres from Moscow. When the Empire was broken up in 1945, a large portion of Berlin became part of the newly formed state of West Germany. But Berlin was separated from West Germany, and totally surrounded by the German Democratic Republic (East Germany), which had been founded at the same time.

These two post-war German states have had frequent disagreements over the years, and West Berlin has often found itself cut off from the rest of West Germany. After one crucial disagreement, in 1948, it woke to find all roads and railway lines into the city had been closed by the DDR. The only way in or out of the city was by plane, and so British and American airforces had to run an emergency air service to carry people, food, petrol and even coal into the besieged city.

Since then, the two German states have become more friendly. But even today, West Berlin can only be reached by crossing territory belonging to the DDR. Aircraft must use particular lanes when flying over DDR territory to reach West Berlin's international airport at Tempelhof. And West Berliners are only allowed to travel on certain motorways and railway routes between their home and the rest of West Germany. Even on these routes, travellers to and from the city must carry a passport and a visa giving permission to travel through the DDR.

The Berlin wall

Today, West Berlin is divided from the DDR by a high concrete wall. This is more than a simple boundary to show where one country ends and another begins. It is an impassable frontier, backed by electric fences, watch-towers and armed guards. These are all designed to prevent anyone leaving the DDR without permission.

When this Berlin Wall was built in 1961 it split the old imperial capital in two. Overnight, West Berliners were separated from their main shops,

The Berlin wall, which divides West Berlin from East Germany.

Night view of the Europa centre at the end of the Kurfürstendam.

cathedral, council offices, and even from their main tram depot. The wall divided West Berlin from the eastern half of the city, West Germany from the DDR, and many West Berliners from family and friends in the East.

At first, the wall was a crude affair. It was built overnight from any materials that came to hand, and was topped by coils of rusty barbed wire. Over the years, the wall has been rebuilt several times and has become a strange tourist attraction.

While no longer the capital of West Germany, West Berlin is still the home of more than two million people. At its heart the wide, tree-lined avenue of the Kurfürstendam is surrounded by luxury hotels, crowded shops and all types of exciting entertainments. The city also boasts a world-famous zoo and aquarium, rolling green pine forests, and shimmering lakes. Life here is very different indeed from that in East Berlin.

The Berlin underground
If you take a trip on the Berlin underground, on the line between Mariendorf and Tegel, you will get a strange feeling of travelling back in time. Leaving West Berlin at Kochstrasse station, you will pass directly beneath East Berlin. Although the train rumbles through several stations, it won't stop. They have been closed to passengers for many years. Now they are dim and dusty. The clocks have all stopped, and the posters advertise long forgotten plays and concerts. The stations have been left just as they were on the 31st August 1961, when the city was divided and the Berlin Wall had just been begun.

Index and summary

Area:	248,651 kilometres
Population:	61,321,700 (approx)
Capital:	Bonn
Main towns:	Berlin (West), Hamburg, Munich, Cologne, Essen, Frankfurt am Main
Federal states:	Schleswig-Holstein, Hamburg, Lower Saxony, Bremen, North-Rhine Westphalia, Hessen, Rhineland Palatinate, Baden-Württemberg, Bavari Saarland, Berlin (West)
Main exports:	Machinery, cars, chemicals, iron and steel, textiles
Main imports:	Petroleum and coking coal, manufactured goods, raw materials
Main crops:	Barley, wheat, oats, rye
Highest point:	Zugspitze, 2965 metres
Longest river:	the Rhine
Official language:	German
Currency:	100 Pfennigs to 1 Deutsch Mark
National airline:	Lufthansa